Famous Forts Throughout American History™

Fort Laramie

Charles W. Maynard

The Rosen Publishing Group's
PowerKids Press™
New York

For David, Hal, Elizabeth, and Dan—always friends

Published in 2002 by The Rosen Publishing Group, Inc.
29 East 21st Street, New York, NY 10010

Copyright © 2002 by The Rosen Publishing Group, Inc.

All rights reserved. No part of this book may be reproduced in any form without permission in writing from the publisher, except by a reviewer.

First Edition

Book Design: Michael Caroleo   Layout Assistance: Nick Sciacca

Project Editor: Kathy Campbell

Photo Credits: p. 1 © Dave G. Houser/CORBIS; p. 4 © The Walters Art Museum, Baltimore; pp. 7, 8, 12 (Laramie remains), 16, 19 © Lowell Georgia/CORBIS; p. 11 © Bettmann/CORBIS; p. 12 (marching) © Craig Aurness/CORBIS; pp. 12 (Sioux treaty), 15 (Sioux attack), 20 © CORBIS; p. 15 (buffalo hunter) © Geoffrey Clements/CORBIS; pp. 16 (man in cavalry uniform firing cannon), 19 (woman washing laundry) © James L. Amos/CORBIS.

Maynard, Charles W. (Charles William), 1955–
  Fort Laramie / Charles W. Maynard.—1st ed.
      p. cm. — (Famous forts throughout American history)
Includes bibliographical references (p.   ) and index.
  ISBN 13: 978-1-4358-3674-7
 1. Fort Laramie (Wyo. : Fort)—History—Juvenile literature. 2. Frontier and pioneer life—Wyoming—Juvenile literature. 3. Frontier and pioneer life—West (U.S.)—Juvenile literature. 4. West (U.S.)—History—To 1848—Juvenile literature. 5. West (U.S.)—History—1848–1860—Juvenile literature. 6. Fort Laramie National Historic site (Wyo.)—Juvenile literature. [1. Fort Laramie (Wyo. : Fort)] I. Title.
  F769.F6 M27 2002
  978.7'18—dc21

00–013206

Manufactured in the United States of America

Contents

1	Fort William	5
2	Trails West	6
3	The Army Takes Over	9
4	Moving the Mail	10
5	A Military Post	13
6	Native American Neighbors	14
7	A Soldier's Life	17
8	Families at Fort Laramie	18
9	Going West	21
10	Visiting Fort Laramie Today	22
	Glossary	23
	Index	24
	Web Sites	24

American artist Alfred Jacob Miller visited the trading post of Fort William in 1837. He painted many images of the fort and of Native Americans, such as these Oglala, who camped outside the fort to trade.

Fort William

Fur trappers in search of beavers traveled west in the 1820s and 1830s. Fur companies built forts for trading posts where Native Americans and trappers brought the **pelts** to trade for supplies and money.

In the summer of 1834, William Sublette and his company of fur trappers built a fort on the banks of the Laramie River in today's Wyoming. Squared cottonwood logs laid upright in a trench, or ditch, formed the walls of the rectangular fort. **Blockhouses** perched atop opposite corners and over the gate provided protection. Inside the fort, small huts lined the wall. A large, two-story building across from the gate housed the head trader and the store. Artist Alfred Jacob Miller visited Fort William in 1837 and painted some of the only existing pictures of the fort.

Trails West

Fort William had rich grass, thick cottonwood groves, and clear water. The fort was an important stopping place for many settlers moving to the Far West. Native Americans first used the trails that later were traveled by white settlers. The Oregon, Mormon, and California Trails passed the fort.

Narcissa Whitman and Eliza Spalding were the first white women to visit the fort on their journey to Oregon in 1836. By 1841, the rotting wooden fort was **abandoned** and replaced by an **adobe** brick fort, called Fort John. More and more people stopped at the new fort to repair their wagons, buy supplies, or rest during the long, hard journey to the West.

The Mormons were a group of people who moved in 1846 to present-day Utah. The Mormons sought freedom to practice their religious beliefs. Mormons

Today park rangers at Fort Laramie dress in clothing of the 1800s as part of a living history program. This ranger shows visitors what daily life was like for women and soldiers' wives who stayed at the fort during the 1840s, when the Oregon Trail made it a popular stop.

often stopped at Fort John to restock their supplies before going on to Utah. The fort was also an important supply post for the thousands of people trying to get to California in the 1850s after gold was discovered there.

Today visitors can see for themselves how the officers' quarters at Fort Laramie looked during the second half of the nineteenth century. The fort became a military base after 1849, when travelers on the Oregon Trail needed protection during conflicts with Native Americans.

The Army Takes Over

The American Fur Company owned old Fort William. The newer adobe fort, built in 1841, was first called Fort John and later was renamed Fort Laramie for the Laramie River that flowed by its brick walls.

In 1849, the U.S. Army bought the fort to better protect the many settlers who traveled west on the trails. The U.S. Army continued to use the adobe brick fort but started to build other buildings nearby. One of the first buildings to be constructed was a large building that would house officers. This building was later called Old **Bedlam**. Some think the name Bedlam comes from the many loud parties the officers held there.

Fort Laramie no longer served only as a trading post. It also housed **cavalry** and **infantry**. The soldiers tried to keep the peace between the settlers on the trails and the Native Americans who lived in the area.

The trading post at Fort Laramie is stocked with some of the goods that people during the 1800s might have bought. Travelers needed to restock their supplies before continuing their journey to the West.

Moving the Mail

In the 1850s, mail took anywhere from six weeks to six months to reach California from the eastern United States. People in the West wanted faster mail routes. On April 3, 1860, the **Pony Express** began carrying mail between California and Missouri. Fort Laramie was one of 190 stations where riders exchanged horses as they carried the mail in saddlebags. By using the Pony Express, the mail could cross the country in 10 to 12 days, following the route of the California Trail. The completion of the first **telegraph** line across the country, in October 1861, caused the Pony Express to quit carrying the mail because messages could be telegraphed faster and cheaper.

Stagecoaches also followed the same route and used Fort Laramie as a station. Once each week, the stagecoaches came to Fort Laramie on a 12-day journey from Missouri. Dusty trails, outlaws, and raiding Native Americans made the trip difficult and dangerous.

A Pony Express rider quickly takes the mail to the next stop on the route between St. Joseph, Missouri, and Sacramento, California. Pony Express riders stopped at Fort Laramie from 1860 to 1861.

Men who are dressed in U.S. Army uniforms from the late 1860s march in a program that celebrates Fort Laramie's living history. The Army bought the trading post Fort John in 1849 and renamed it Fort Laramie.

A Military Post

In the years after the Civil War (1861–1865), Fort Laramie became a **military** center for U.S. Army activity. The **garrison** increased in number. The old adobe fort was a small part of the larger Fort Laramie. After the adobe fort crumbled, the newer fort had no walls but was a collection of buildings grouped around a large parade ground. The flag fluttered at the top of a high flagpole in the constant wind of the Wyoming plains. The troops drilled on the parade ground, raising dust as they marched. Only once did anyone attack Fort Laramie. In the summer of 1864, a band of **Sioux** warriors raided it to steal some of the Army's horses.

Native Americans no longer came to Fort Laramie to trade furs but to make peace. Soldiers and chiefs gathered there to talk about how everyone could live peacefully in the West. In 1851, and in 1868, several Native American nations signed two important **treaties**.

Bottom Left: *The ruins of the adobe fort can be seen today at Fort Laramie.*
Bottom Right: *Lieutenant General William T. Sherman of the U.S. Army and members of the Sioux nation sign a treaty at Fort Laramie in 1868.*

Native American Neighbors

The Sioux visited the original fort frequently after its construction in 1834. They lived on the Great Plains and hunted **bison**. The bison, also called buffalo, satisfied many of the Sioux's needs. The Native Americans ate the meat and built shelters from the buffalo hides. The Sioux also made robes and blankets from the bison furs for warmth in the harsh winters on the Great Plains. They traded extra hides for supplies at Fort Laramie.

As the fur trade ended and more settlers came, the Sioux and other Native American nations were made angry by so many people crossing and claiming their land. They fought to keep the **territory** where they lived and hunted. Soldiers at Fort Laramie tried to keep the peace between the Native Americans and the settlers.

Top: *Sioux warriors attacked settlers who decided to build homes on the Great Plains. Some Native American nations became angry when many settlers began to claim the land.*
Bottom: *For most Native Americans on the plains, hunting buffalo was a way of life. Settlers and white hunters affected these Native Americans' means of staying alive when they began to kill buffalo in large numbers.*

A soldier fires a cannon during a program for visitors at Fort Laramie.

A Soldier's Life

Soldiers sent to Fort Laramie found life there difficult. Regular drills for the men, horses, and **equipment** filled a large part of each day. "**Fatigue** duties," which were chores to keep the fort in good repair, took up much time. The cavalry exercised and **groomed** horses while the infantry cleaned their guns and practiced shooting.

Discipline at Fort Laramie was harsh. Severe penalties followed the breaking of even minor rules, such as fighting or not completing assigned work. Punishment sometimes meant staying in a bare, unheated guardhouse. Some men grew tired of this life and ran away. Others, like Sergeant Leodegar Schnyder who served at Fort Laramie for 37 years, liked the routines and stayed for a long time.

These cavalrymen are watering their horses near Fort Laramie. Company K of the Third Cavalry lived at Fort Laramie in 1876. In addition to the cavalry, the Seventh Infantry served at the fort in the 1880s.

Families at Fort Laramie

The wives and children of officers were also a part of life at Fort Laramie. Officers usually sent their children back East to school. Most of the other soldiers' children attended school at the fort. A soldier taught the youngsters their lessons. When the children were not in school, perhaps they played along the banks of the Laramie River or among the **ruins** of old Fort John.

Weddings, holidays, and the visits of generals were special occasions. Christmas Day, December 25, and Independence Day, July 4, meant **decorations** and dinners. Women tried to make the stark buildings of Fort Laramie into comfortable homes. Some of what we know today about life in **frontier** forts comes to us from letters that women wrote to their relatives back East and from their **journals**.

Top: A soldier's bedroom at Fort Laramie has been rebuilt so visitors can learn about how officers and soldiers lived at the Army outpost. Bottom: A woman washes clothes during a tour to show today's visitors how soldiers' wives and families lived at the frontier fort.

"June 8, 1864. This morning all was bustle and hurry.... The stars and stripes were proudly floating over it [Fort Laramie]. At the sight of which brought forth cheer after cheer from the throats of hundreds of ... men, women and children, who all know and feel what true patriotism means."

Harriet A. Loughary

Timeline

1834 William Sublette and fur traders build Fort William.
1836 Fort William is bought by the American Fur Company.
1841 Fort William is replaced by Fort John.
1843-48 Thousands of people travel the Oregon and Mormon Trails.
1849 The U.S. Army buys Fort John and officially renames it Fort Laramie.
1851 A large council meets at Fort Laramie to sign a treaty.

1860-1861 The Pony Express runs through Fort Laramie.
1868 The Treaty of Fort Laramie is signed.
1890 Fort Laramie is decommissioned, or removed from service.
1938 On July 16, Fort Laramie is proclaimed a National Monument.
1960 On April 29, Fort Laramie is converted to a National Historic Site.

Going West

As people moved to the Far West in the 1800s, thousands of them passed through Fort Laramie. During its 56-year history, the fort served as an important stopping place for the people who traveled to places such as Oregon and California. The fort had a blacksmith, a wagon maker's shop, and three bakeries. As the number of people who stopped at Fort Laramie increased, relations between the travelers and the Native Americans became difficult. Fort Laramie grew from a trading post to an important military fort on the frontier when the U.S. Army bought the fort in 1849 to help protect the travelers.

Fort Laramie, founded in 1834 as Fort William, is shown here in a nineteenth-century illustration. It began as a trading post, especially for beaver skins and bison hides. Next, people traveling on the Oregon Trail used the fort as a supply stop. It became a military fort in 1849. People inside the fort had a clear view across the plains, making it difficult for anyone to take the fort by surprise.

Visiting Fort Laramie Today

The National Park Service preserves Fort Laramie for all to enjoy and learn about its history. Park rangers talk about the days when the fur trade, the Pony Express, and the soldiers made Fort Laramie a major stronghold in the West. Some rangers dress in the clothing and uniforms of the 1800s to show what life in the fort was like. Eleven of the fort's original buildings have been **restored**. The oldest preserved building is Old Bedlam. The U.S. flag still flies over the parade ground.

Scott's Bluff in Nebraska and Register Cliff in Wyoming are nearby sites that remind visitors of the many people who came by Fort Laramie on their way to the West. The ruts made by wagon wheels on the Oregon Trail are still visible in soft stone near the fort. The National Park Service continues to study the fort's history with **archaeological** digs and research into old records. Fort Laramie National Historic Site, along with nearby sites, helps people today learn about the great movement of settlers who traveled west in the 1800s.

Glossary

abandoned (uh-BAN-dund) To have left something without planning to come back.
adobe (uh-DOH-bee) Brick made from dried mud and straw.
archaeological (ar-kee-o-LOJ-ih-kul) Having to do with studying the life and culture of earlier times.
bedlam (BED-lum) Full of noise and confusion.
bison (BY-son) A wild ox, also called a buffalo, which once roamed the plains of the United States.
blockhouses (BLOK-hows-ez) Buildings of heavy logs that have holes in the walls from which to shoot weapons.
cavalry (KA-vul-ree) The part of the army that rides horses.
decorations (deh-kuh-RAY-shunz) Ornaments put up for a special occasion.
equipment (uh-KWIP-mint) All of the supplies needed to do an activity.
fatigue (fuh-TEEG) Hard labor or being worn out and tired.
frontier (frun-TEER) The edge of a settled country, where the wilderness begins.
garrison (GAR-ih-sun) Troops stationed at a fort.
groomed (GROOMD) An activity that included cleaning a horse.
infantry (IN-fun-tree) The part of an army that walks while fighting.
journals (JER-nuhlz) Notebooks in which people write their thoughts.
military (MIH-lih-ter-ee) Part of a government that protects the United States; the armed forces, such as the army.
pelts (PELTS) Animal skins with the fur still attached.
Pony Express (POH-nee ek-SPRES) The mail service used from 1860 to 1861, in which riders carried mail across the western part of the United States.
restored (reh-STORD) When something has been brought back to its original state.
ruins (ROO-enz) Something that is damaged badly.
Sioux (SOO) A Native American nation that lived on the Great Plains in the 1700s and 1800s.
telegraph (TEL-eh-graf) A system for sending messages with electric impulses sent over wire.
territory (TEHR-uh-tor-ee) Land that is controlled by a person or a group of people.
treaties (TREE-teez) Formal agreements, especially between nations, signed and agreed upon by each nation.

Index

A
American Fur Company, 9

B
blockhouses, 5

F
families at Fort Laramie, 18
fatigue duties, 17
Fort John, 6, 9, 18
Fort Laramie National Historic Site, 22
Fort William, 5, 6, 9
fur trappers, 5

M
Miller, Alfred Jacob, 5
Mormons, 6

N
Native Americans, 5, 6, 9, 10, 13, 14, 21

O
Old Bedlam, 9, 22

P
Pony Express, 10, 22

R
Register Cliff, 22

S
Scott's Bluff, 22
Sioux, 13, 14
stagecoaches, 10
Sublette, William, 5

T
telegraph line, 10
treaties, 13

Web Sites

To learn more about Fort Laramie, check out these Web sites:
www.fortlaramie.com
www.isu.edu/~trinmich/Oregontrail.html
www.OCTA-trails.org

www.ingramcontent.com/pod-product-compliance
Lightning Source LLC
Chambersburg PA
CBHW041121070526
44584CB00002B/237